Andrew Jackson

History Maker Bios

Carol H. Behrman

BARNES
&NOBLE
B O O K S
NEW YORK

To my dear Rose—C. H. B.

Thanks to Staff of The Hermitage,
Home of President Andrew Jackson,
for its assistance with this book.

Illustrations by Tim Parlin

Text copyright © 2005 by Carol H. Behrman
Illustrations copyright © 2005 by Lerner Publications Company

This 2005 edition published by Barnes & Noble Publishing, Inc.,
by arrangement with Lerner Publications Company,
a division of Lerner Publishing Group, Minneapolis, MN.

Barnes & Noble Publishing, Inc.
122 Fifth Avenue
New York, NY 10011

ISBN: 0-7607-4027-5

Printed in the United States of America

04 05 06 07 08 MCH 10 9 8 7 6 5 4 3 2 1

Table of Contents

INTRODUCTION

Andrew Jackson grew up on the American frontier as the son of poor farmers. He was a wild, fun-loving boy who often got into trouble. No one ever dreamed that he would be a great man someday. But Andy surprised them all. He became a brave general whose soldiers nicknamed him Old Hickory for his strength and courage. After he led the U.S. Army to victory at the Battle of New Orleans during the War of 1812 against Great Britain, he was called the Hero of New Orleans. Later, he served as the seventh president of the United States. But throughout his life, Andrew Jackson always remembered growing up poor. He fought for the plain, common folks, and they loved him.

This is his story.

1 A FRONTIER BOYHOOD

Andy Jackson's mother and father, Elizabeth and Andrew, were immigrants from Ireland. When they came across the Atlantic Ocean in 1765, before Andy was born, there was no United States. Great Britain owned the American colonies.

The Jacksons and their two sons, two-year-old Hugh and five-month-old Robert, settled in the Waxhaws, a region in western North Carolina. Life was not easy on the frontier. The land was barren and scrubby—not good at all for farming. The Jacksons worked hard, but tragedy struck in February 1767. Andrew was badly hurt and died. One month later, on March 15, Elizabeth's third son was born. She named the boy Andrew after his father.

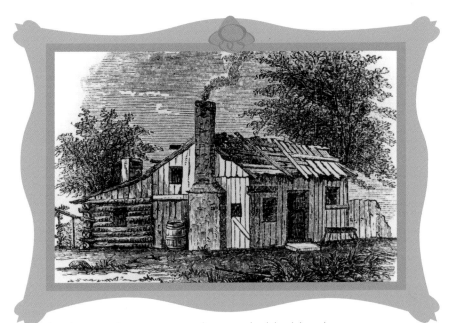

Andy was born in a cabin probably like this one on March 15, 1767.

Baby Andy and his brothers went with Elizabeth to live with their Aunt Jane and her family at their farm. Andy's mother helped take care of the family and the house. Everyone had lots of chores to do, but Andy worked hard and never complained. He didn't mind farmwork.

THE WAXHAWS

When Andy Jackson grew up in the Waxhaws, not many people lived in this wild, rough place on North Carolina's western frontier. Bears and other wild animals roamed the woods. Boys learned to use guns at a young age. They hunted and fished to help feed their families. Many Native Americans also lived in the region. Their homes had been there before the white settlers had come, and sometimes they fought with settlers. All in all, life in the Waxhaws was dangerous. Its people had to be tough and independent.

Andy went to school in a one-room house like this one.

School was a different matter. The small schoolhouse that Andy went to had one room for students of all ages. There were no windows and no chairs. The children sat on logs. Andy would rather play with his friends than sit in the schoolroom. He often skipped class. He loved to wrestle and to ride horses. He was good at most games and usually won. But even when he was losing, Andy never gave up.

Andy read a notice about the Declaration of Independence (LEFT). The declaration said that the American colonies were free of British rule.

Andy also loved to play tricks on his pals, but sometimes he got angry when he was the butt of a joke. Once, when his friends made fun of him, he shouted, "By God, if one of you laughs, I'll kill him!"

Andy was popular despite his temper. And he was very good at one school subject: reading. Even many grown-ups could not read then. By the time Andy was nine, townspeople would gather around to hear him read the news. One summer day in 1776, he read an important notice about a Declaration of Independence.

Many people in the American colonies did not want to belong to Great Britain anymore. In the Declaration of Independence, a group of American leaders said that the colonies were free from British rule. People cheered at the words, "All men are created equal."

Americans were ready to fight for their freedom. The British would not give up their colonies without a war. Men from the Waxhaws and from all over the colonies joined the Continental Army, a force led by General George Washington.

General George Washington led the men of the Continental Army against the British during the American Revolution (1775–1783).

Sparking the American Revolution

Great Britain's king ruled the American colonies, and he did not treat his American subjects well. He forced them to pay taxes that Americans called unfair, put them in prison if they objected, and sent soldiers to enforce his laws. Some colonists, called patriots, demanded justice, but the king ignored their requests. The colonists began to talk about separating from Great Britain. In 1776, leaders from all the colonies met in Philadelphia, Pennsylvania, and declared their independence. But before America could be free, a war had to be fought and won.

Andy and his friends wanted to fight the British too. But they were too young to go to war, so they pretended to be soldiers. The boys played with swords and rifles made from sticks. They longed to be old enough to really fight.

But real war was ugly. The British army won most of the battles at first, and many Americans died. In May 1780, Andy's oldest brother, Hugh, was killed. It was a terrible, sad day for the Jackson family.

Years of bloody war followed. Meanwhile, Andy grew tall and strong. When he was thirteen, he and his brother Robert joined the fight. Andy delivered important messages for officers in the Continental Army. He was proud to be a soldier at last.

Andy's brother Hugh died after this battle in South Carolina in 1780.

Then war came to the Waxhaws. When the British attacked their town, Andy and Robert had to escape into the woods. They hid all night long. But the next morning, British soldiers captured the boys.

When a British officer ordered Andy to polish his boots, Andy refused. He said that he was a prisoner of war, not a servant.

The officer's face turned red with anger. He raised his sword, and Andy threw up a hand to protect himself. The sword gashed his fingers and head as it came down. But Andy still wouldn't polish the officer's boots.

Andy refused to shine a British officer's boots. His act of bravery and pride nearly cost him his life.

Andy and Robert were thrown into a dirty, crowded prison, where they both became sick with smallpox. When their mother heard what had happened, she traveled many miles to plead with the British for the boys' freedom.

She convinced a British officer to release her sons. Robert died on the long, miserable journey home, and Andy was ill for a long time. "I was a skeleton," he said, but his mother tenderly nursed him back to health.

When Andy was well enough, his mother went to nurse other soldiers in Charleston, South Carolina. As she worked on ships crowded with ill and injured men, she caught the disease cholera. She died in 1781.

Andy never forgot his mother's words before she had left for Charleston. She had reminded him that he must always be honest and loyal. "Never tell a lie nor take what is not your own," he remembered her saying. Andy Jackson was fourteen years old. He was all alone in the world.

2 THE WILD YOUNG REBEL

After six years of war, the fighting in the American Revolution finally ended in 1781. The Americans had won. The British soldiers went home, and the colonies were free. Bells rang and people cheered in all the thirteen states.

Andy was proud of his part in the fight for freedom. But his mother and brothers were gone. He was lonely and confused. His relatives tried to help by taking Andy into their homes, but he never stayed long. He quarreled with everyone and hung out with a wild group of friends. They played cards and bet on horse races. Andy and his teenage pals were rowdy and careless. One of these friends described Andy, saying, "No boy ever lived who liked fun better than he."

American colonists cheer the news of their victory over the British.

It seemed to many people as though Andy Jackson had no ambition. He owed money everywhere and was in deep trouble. But his mother's teachings had not been in vain. Andy soon realized he was wasting his life. He decided to go back to school and make something of himself.

Andy worked as a teacher for a short time, but soon he was ready for something new. He decided to become a lawyer. Andy could learn the law if he could find a licensed attorney with whom to work and study.

A DICEY PASTIME

One of Andy's risky habits was playing a dice game called Rattle and Snap. Andy often bet—and lost—money on the game. Once, when he was close to going to jail for his debts, he took one last chance. He bet his horse—his only valuable possession—and won. Andy paid off his debts and never played another round of dice.

Andy learned the law by studying it in a law office like this one in Salisbury, North Carolina.

Andy went to the large town of Salisbury, North Carolina. An important local attorney named Spruce McCay agreed to let Andy work for him and learn the law.

Andy studied with McCay for two years. He worked hard, but he also had time to find new friends. Once again, he became the leader of a fun-loving crowd. He was popular with both young men and young women. Andy was tall and handsome, with striking blue eyes and thick red hair.

In September 1787, Andrew Jackson finished his studies. Two judges tested him on his knowledge of the law. Andrew passed the test easily. At the age of twenty, he was officially qualified to work as a lawyer.

But there were already many lawyers in Salisbury. Andrew decided his chances of finding work were better somewhere else. He heard about a job opening for a lawyer in the Western District, an area that stretched westward to the Mississippi River. It was a rough, tough place, and many people were afraid to travel there. Andrew took the job. He was tough too. After all, he had grown up on the frontier.

Andrew set out on horseback with a few friends. He took along a rifle, two pistols, and his hunting dogs. Law books were stuffed into his pack. Andrew was on his way to take on the lawbreakers of the Western District.

3 LAW COMES TO TENNESSEE

Jackson's group headed for Nashville, a city in a part of the Western District that was later called Tennessee. The trip was long and dangerous. The travelers crossed over mountains and through wild, unfamiliar land.

Jackson stands armed and ready to uphold the law on the frontier

When they reached Nashville in 1788, it wasn't much of a town. It had only a few shabby stores, and the courthouse was falling apart. Even worse, some people didn't respect the law. But Jackson made sure that people obeyed the law—and that those who didn't paid for it. Once a criminal stamped hard on Jackson's foot. Jackson didn't hesitate. He swung a block of wood at the man and knocked him out.

The people of Nashville welcomed the tough new prosecutor. Soon the young lawyer had lots of business. He also had a comfortable new home. He rented rooms from the Donelsons, an important Nashville family. Jackson liked the Donelsons, especially their beautiful daughter, Rachel. She was living at home after leaving her husband. She and Andrew became friends and soon fell in love. They were married in August 1791. In 1794, they remarried after learning that their first marriage wasn't official.

Andrew met his wife, Rachel Donelson, during his stay in Nashville.

The busy U.S. capital city, Philadelphia, as it looked in about 1796

Twenty-four-year-old Jackson had a successful career and a loving wife. Eventually, he and Rachel developed a fine home and farm called the Hermitage. Meanwhile, the area around Nashville was growing, and in 1796, Tennessee became a state. The new state needed strong leaders. Jackson was elected to the House of Representatives in the U.S. Congress. He traveled to Philadelphia—the country's capital at that time—for meetings and government business.

It was important work. But Andrew was unhappy, and he missed Rachel.

Jackson left his job as a representative in 1797. But a few months later, he was back in Philadelphia as a senator. Jackson was glad to serve his country, but he still missed Rachel, and he needed to return to his law practice. In 1798, he quit and hurried home.

In 1804, Jackson made his home at the Hermitage.

Judge Jackson (POINTING) orders a disrespectful criminal to give himself up. A crowd of Nashville residents looks on.

Back in Nashville, Jackson was elected a judge. He took his new job very seriously. He told his juries to always "do what is right," and he kept up his tough reputation. A criminal once seized a gun and cursed at the judge and jury before charging out of the courthouse. Judge Jackson acted quickly. He stormed into the street after the man and flashed pistols in his face. "Surrender," he ordered, "or I'll blow you through." The man dropped his gun.

Jackson's quick temper flared up whenever he felt wronged. To defend his honor, he sometimes challenged men to gunfights. Jackson fought one duel after he became major general of the Tennessee militia, or state army. Another man who had wanted the job was angry. He insulted Andrew and Rachel. At the duel, both men drew their pistols. Fortunately, friends settled the fight before a single shot was fired.

But in 1806, a duel ended badly. Jackson won, but he killed the other man and was badly wounded himself. The duel left him with a bullet in his chest for the rest of his life, causing him great pain.

Jackson, wounded during a duel in 1806, shot and killed his rival.

Jackson and Rachel adopted their nephew Andrew in 1809. They named him Andrew Jackson Jr.

Andrew was happy and respected during these years. Just one thing was missing. He and Rachel had no children. In 1809, Andrew and Rachel adopted one of her brother's babies and named him Andrew Jackson Jr. They were thrilled to have a child.

Meanwhile, the United States was having trouble with an old enemy. In 1812, the young country found itself at war with Great Britain again.

4 GENERAL JACKSON

Even after the Revolution, Great Britain tried to treat the United States like a colony. U.S. ships weren't safe at sea. Captured U.S. sailors were forced to join the British navy. In the War of 1812, the new country fought for its rights again.

At first, the British were winning the war. They burned down the President's House in Washington, D.C., and captured other cities. Things looked bad for the United States.

Andrew Jackson had fought for his country as a teenager, and he wanted to help again. General Jackson called upon young men in Tennessee to join him. The men respected Jackson, and many were ready to follow him into battle.

The British attacked the new capital city of Washington, D.C., during the War of 1812.

This 1815 painting is one of the first known pictures of Jackson. It shows how Major General Jackson looked when he led his men to New Orleans during the War of 1812.

Jackson's troops waited months for orders. Finally, they were told to head to New Orleans. As people cheered and waved from shore on an icy December day, Jackson and his soldiers boarded riverboats and sailed to Natchez, Mississippi. They set up camp and waited for supplies, but none came. They ran out of food and medicine. The men were hungry and sick.

New orders finally came—telling Jackson to go home and to leave his troops to manage for themselves. General Jackson was angry. He would never abandon his men.

Jackson offered his horse to his men during their journey back to Tennessee.

Jackson led his ragged army on a tough five-hundred-mile trek. He gave his horse to sick men and told stories to keep their spirits up. Jackson's soldiers were grateful to their courageous general. They called him Old Hickory, because hickory wood was strong. After bringing his men safely home, Jackson was a local hero. One newspaper wrote, "Long will [their] General live in the memory of . . . West Tennessee."

In October 1813, Jackson finally got the chance to lead troops in battle. He was ordered to fight the Creek people, who were helping the British. Bloody battles followed, where hundreds of Creeks and many U.S. soldiers were killed. In 1814, U.S. forces won the Creek War, and General Jackson made the Creeks give up much of their land. The Creeks feared Jackson and called him Sharp Knife. However, Jackson could show pity as well as fierceness. He and Rachel adopted Lyncoya, a young Creek boy whose family had been killed in the war.

Jackson talks about a peace agreement with Creek leader Red Eagle. The Creek people called Jackson Sharp Knife.

Meanwhile, the British were nearing New Orleans. This important city's defenses were weak, and most people didn't think it stood a chance against Britain's powerful forces. But Jackson was determined to save the city. He traveled to New Orleans and began making plans for battle.

The British invaded in December 1814 with more soldiers and more guns than the U.S. forces had. But Jackson was not afraid, roaring, "I will smash them!" On January 8, 1815, the British attacked. Jackson's men were good shots, and they fired on the British troops from behind dirt walls.

Jackson (STANDING CENTER) leads his men against the British during the Battle of New Orleans in 1815.

General Jackson was called the Hero of New Orleans for his fearless leadership during the Battle of New Orleans.

The British were surprised by the Americans' skill in battle. Hundreds of British soldiers died, and the troops finally retreated. The United States had won the battle.

New Orleans held a grand parade to honor General Jackson. People across the country called him the Hero of New Orleans.

After the war, forty-eight-year-old Jackson was glad to go home to the Hermitage and his beloved Rachel. He settled down to care for his family and his farm.

But the general's skills were needed again. In 1817, the U.S. government asked him to capture land from the Seminole people in Florida. Spain owned Florida at the time, but Jackson's troops defeated the Seminoles and took control of the area. Spain sold Florida to the United States, and Americans called Jackson a hero.

In 1821, Jackson became Florida's governor. He and Rachel moved there, and Jackson worked to make laws that protected the people. But the Jacksons didn't like Florida, and they went home as soon as the new government was running well. They ran their farm and welcomed many visitors. Jackson hoped to spend the rest of his life there. But his country would need him one more time.

5 PRESIDENT OF THE PEOPLE

The Jackson family had a big house and a prosperous farm. Life was easy at the Hermitage. But Jackson never forgot what it was like to grow up poor, and he worried that the government helped the rich and powerful too much. Someone had to protect the rest of the people. In 1828, at the age of sixty-one, Jackson ran for president.

Many powerful people didn't like Jackson and didn't want him to be president. Newspapers printed unkind things about him and Rachel. But the common people wanted him as their leader and elected him the seventh president of the United States.

It was time for the Jacksons to move to the President's House. But Rachel had been very ill, and the nasty remarks about her and Jackson had upset her terribly. Her health grew worse and worse. Just after the election, she had a heart attack. She died with her husband at her bedside. Jackson could not believe his beloved wife was gone.

Rachel was buried in the garden of the Hermitage. Jackson's heart was broken. But he had a job to do for his country.

On March 4, 1829, Jackson was sworn in as president. As the "people's president," he invited the public to the celebration. Thousands of people came, crowding the elegant President's House and getting it dirty with their muddy boots. But these were the people who had elected President Jackson, and he vowed to do all he could to help them and to make the nation strong.

Thousands of people came to cheer their new president.

Not all of Jackson's decisions were good for everyone. For example, like many Americans at the time, he didn't believe that Native Americans deserved the same rights as white people. In 1830, to please white settlers who wanted Native American land, Jackson signed the Indian Removal Act. The act forced Native American families to move westward across the Mississippi River. The trip was long and hard, and thousands of Native Americans died. This tragic journey became known as the Trail of Tears.

Native Americans move westward under order of Jackson's Indian Removal Act. The journey is called the Trail of Tears.

STATES' RIGHTS

President Jackson struggled with an issue called states' rights. Some southerners said that they shouldn't have to follow federal laws if they didn't agree with them. They claimed that the rights of the states were more important than the demands of the national government. But Jackson knew that the country would weaken if each state could obey some laws but not others. Jackson told southerners, "Our Union . . . must be preserved."

But President Jackson did all he could to help the common people and make the nation strong. He was reelected in 1832. During his eight years in office, he cut spending and paid off the national debt. He also tried to make the country bigger by adding the territory of Texas, then owned by Mexico. He failed. But American settlement in Texas continued.

This political cartoon shows Jackson closing the Bank of the United States. He called the bank a monster and crushed it.

Jackson faced one of his toughest challenges in his second term. He thought that the Bank of the United States was too big and powerful. Instead of this central bank, he wanted local banks for ordinary people around the country. He fought to close down the bank, and he finally won.

Jackson believed that, as the country's leader, he had a "sacred trust" to carry out the will of the people. He worked hard at that job, and Americans were grateful. When Jackson's presidency ended in 1837, he was the most popular president since George Washington. At seventy years of age, it was time for the old soldier to go home.

During Jackson's last years at the Hermitage, his old wounds often hurt him, and he had difficulty breathing. As always, he bravely ignored the pain. He still read newspapers and kept up with the country's affairs. He gave advice to new leaders, and visitors came from far and wide to see the great man. People respectfully called him "General."

The general's health finally gave out. Family and friends surrounded his bed. He told them not to cry, whispering, "We shall all meet in Heaven." Andrew Jackson died on June 8, 1845. The people's president was buried beside Rachel at the Hermitage.

This photograph of Jackson was taken in 1844 or 1845, near the end of his life. His successful time as president is often called the Age of Jackson.

TIMELINE

In the year . . .

1780	Andrew and his brother Robert were captured by British troops.	Age 13
1781	Robert died of smallpox. Andrew's mother died of cholera.	
1783–84	he taught school in the Waxhaws. he studied law in North Carolina.	Age 17
1788	he arrived in Nashville to work as a prosecutor in the Western District.	Age 21
1791	he and Rachel were married. They remarried in 1794.	
1796	he was elected representative from Tennessee.	Age 29
1797	he was elected senator from Tennessee.	
1798	he was elected a judge in Tennessee.	
1802	he became a major general of the Tennessee militia.	Age 35
1809	he and Rachel adopted Andrew Jackson Jr.	
1812	the War of 1812 began.	
1814	his troops won the Creek War.	
1815	his troops defeated the British at the Battle of New Orleans.	Age 48
1821	he became Florida's governor.	
1828	he was elected U.S. president. Rachel died at the Hermitage.	Age 61
1830	he signed the Indian Removal Act.	
1832	he was reelected president.	Age 65
1845	he died on June 8 and was buried next to Rachel.	Age 78

THE HERMITAGE

Andrew Jackson and Rachel created a beautiful home near Nashville, Tennessee. They named it the Hermitage. It was part of a plantation—a large, southern-style farm—where they grew cotton. Slaves worked on the plantation and in the house. Many Americans believed that slavery was wrong. But Jackson and many other plantation owners disagreed. They depended on slaves to work their fields.

Andrew Jackson lived at the Hermitage for forty years. It was the place he loved best, and he shared many happy times at home with Rachel. "How often," he once said, "do my thoughts lead me back to the Hermitage." Both he and Rachel are buried there in the garden.

Modern tourists can still visit the Hermitage. It is kept just as it was when Jackson lived in it, with the same furniture and pictures on the walls. Jackson's eyeglasses, sword, and Bible are there. So is the special chair he used in his last years when he was ill. Visitors to the Hermitage get an idea of what life was like in the Age of Jackson.

FURTHER READING

Landau, Elaine. *The President's Work: A Look at the Executive Branch.* Minneapolis: Lerner Publications Company, 2004. This book examines how presidents do their job.

Miller, Brandon Marie. *Growing Up in Revolution and the New Nation: 1775 to 1800.* Minneapolis: Lerner Publications Company, 2003. This book for older readers takes a look at life for kids like Andrew Jackson during and after the American Revolution.

Potts, Steve. *Andrew Jackson: A Photo-Illustrated Biography.* Mankato, MN: Bridgestone Books, 1996. This book tells Andrew's story with the help of photos and illustrations.

Sirvaitis, Karen. *Tennessee.* Minneapolis: Lerner Publications Company, 2003. Take a look at the state where Andrew Jackson spent most of his life.

Stefoff, Rebecca. *The War of 1812.* New York: Benchmark Books, 2001. This book explores the War of 1812, including the Battle of New Orleans.

Stein, R. Conrad. *The Trail of Tears.* Chicago: Children's Press, 1993. This book tells of the terrible journey made by Cherokee and other Native Americans after Andrew Jackson signed the Indian Removal Act.

Waxman, Laura Hamilton. *Sequoyah.* Minneapolis: Lerner Publications Company, 2004. Sequoyah was a Cherokee who lived during the time of the Trail of Tears. This biography takes a look at his life.

WEBSITES

Biography of Andrew Jackson
<http://www.whitehouse.gov/history/presidents/aj7.html>
A biography of the seventh president is available at the official White House website.

The Hermitage: Home of President Andrew Jackson
<http://www.thehermitage.com>
This website offers a glimpse into the Hermitage, as well as information on how to visit there.

SELECT BIBLIOGRAPHY

Andrist, Ralph K. *Andrew Jackson, Soldier and Statesman.* New York: American Heritage Publishing Co., 1963.

Davis, Burke. *Old Hickory: A Life of Andrew Jackson.* New York: Dial Press, 1977.

James, Marquis. *The Life of Andrew Jackson, Complete in One Volume.* New York: Bobbs-Merrill Company, 1938.

Remini, Robert V. *Andrew Jackson.* New York: Twayne Publishers, 1966.

Remini, Robert V. *The Life of Andrew Jackson.* New York: Harper and Row, 1988.

Schlesinger, Arthur M., Jr. *The Age of Jackson.* Boston: Little Brown, 1946.

Van Deusen, Glyndon G. *The Jacksonian Era, 1828–1848.* New York: Harper and Row, 1959.

INDEX

Acknowledgments

The images in this book are used with the permission of: Independence National Historical Park, p. 4; Tim Parlin, pp. 6, 14, 16, 21, 29, 37, 44; Tennessee State Museum Photographic Archives, p. 7; © North Wind Picture Archive, pp. 9, 13, 27, 30; courtesy of the National Archives, p. 10; courtesy of the Library of Congress, pp. 11 (LC-USZ62-45172), 17 (LC-USZC2-2131), 22 (LC-USZ62-02630), 26 (LC-USZ62-60870), 32 (LC-USZ62-5244), 34 (LC-USZC4-6222), 39 (LC-USZ62-1805), 42 (LC-USZ62-809), 43 (LC-USZC4-1807), 45 (LC-USZC4-1320); The Hermitage: Home of President Andrew Jackson, Nashville, Tennessee, pp. 14, 23, 25, 28, 33, 38; courtesy of Dover Publications, p. 19; © Brown Brothers, p. 24; Historic Hudson Valley, Tarrytown, New York, p. 31; © Eastern National/courtesy of the Horseshoe Bend National Military Park, p. 35; The Trail of Tears, by Robert Lindneux, Woolaroc Museum, Bartlesville, Oklahoma, p. 40. **Front cover:** courtesy of the Library of Congress (LC-USZC4-2109); illustrations by Tim Parlin. **Back cover:** courtesy of the Library of Congress (LC-USZ61-1453). **For quoted material:** p. 10, 15 (bottom), 26 (top), 41, 43, Marquis James, *The Life of Andrew Jackson, Complete in One Volume* (New York: Bobbs-Merrill Company, 1938); p. 11, *World Book Encyclopedia*, vol. 5, S.V. "Declaration of Independence"; p. 15 (top), Burke Davis, *Old Hickory: A Life of Andrew Jackson* (New York: Dial Press, 1977); p. 17, 26 (bottom), 32, 34, Robert V. Remini, *The Life of Andrew Jackson* (New York: Harper and Row, 1988); p. 42, Robert V. Remini, *Andrew Jackson* (New York: Twayne Publishers, 1966); p. 45, *The Ladies' Hermitage Association, The Hermitage, Home of President Andrew Jackson* (Hermitage, TN: The Ladies' Hermitage Association, 1997).